MW01485483

Love Thy Shadows

By

Maci Taylor

Copyright © 2024 **Maci Taylor**

All rights reserved.

website: **www.macithemystic.com**

Instagram: **The_Alien_Vibe**

Dedication

This book is dedicated to the many initiations and dark nights of the soul that I've had the honor of experiencing throughout this lifetime. Nothing will teach you deeper truths about yourself and life than the dark times. I am so grateful for each moment of darkness that forced me to go within and bring light to every part of my being. The darkness is a truly empowering place if you lean in and let it teach you.

May this book and its entries bring you wisdom and guidance as you navigate your own dark nights of the soul. May you learn to lean into the darkness and allow it to break you down into nothing. May you learn to surrender to the infinite mystery of the universe.

About The Author

Maci Taylor is a cosmic starseed from realms far beyond Earth. She returned to Earth in this lifetime to raise the vibration of the collective consciousness and to teach others how to heal themselves through self-love. She is a gypsy soul who loves traveling and spreading love and light everywhere she goes. She has spent a significant portion of her life going in and out of spiritual initiations and dark times, which has inspired her to find refuge and power in the darkness.

She is a cosmic intuitive, mystic, Shamanic practitioner, and energy alchemist. She currently spends her time helping other souls heal, find their purpose, and activate their gifts. She is also a living testament to the healing power of self-love for the mind, body, and soul. Nothing brings her more joy than helping others on their spiritual journey back home to themselves.

Love Thy Shadows

The EGO **resents** the struggle.

The SOUL **honors** the struggle.

Love Thy Shadows

Each time we release, we become more **free.**

Each time we release, we become more **nothing.**

Each time we release, we become more **everything.**

Love Thy Shadows

How to heal your emotions:

Acknowledge

Honor

Surrender

Release

Transmute

Purify

Liberate

Love Thy Shadows

Every mistake is a life lesson.

Every experience is a life lesson.

You are a student in the classroom of life.

You would not be the divine, empowered soul that you are if your

path had looked any different.

Love Thy Shadows

Life is not a straight line; it's a spiral.
You will always circle back to lessons and
experiences to learn deeper layers of truth.
Healing is not a straight line; it's a spiral.
Your soul will always pull you back toward
experiences and interactions to help you heal
and release deeper layers of self.

Love Thy Shadows

Every situation, interaction, and person
you meet is part of your path.
Every moment is your teacher.

Love Thy Shadows

Pain is the price of freedom.

Pain and suffering are the price of liberation.

You must feel it to heal it.

You must honor the path and everything that comes along with it.

You cannot fully experience immense highs in

life without fully leaning into the lows.

Both deserve your full attention.

Both deserve your light.

Love Thy Shadows

Remember that every tree, every plant, every animal,

and every soul is beautiful and worthy of love,

no matter how tall, skinny, twisted, or fat it is.

And so are you. <3

Love Thy Shadows

All things grow in darkness.

Seeds are planted underground in the darkness of the dirt.

Babies grow in the dark, warm womb.

Caterpillars go into dark cocoons before emerging as butterflies.

Animals go into caves of darkness to hibernate

before awakening in the spring.

All of nature goes through cycles of death and rebirth.

Nothing in nature blooms all year.

The next time you feel like you are in darkness, just remember:

It's time to grow.

Love Thy Shadows

Little by little,

Layer by layer,

We shed and transmute,

Liberating our soul more each time.

Love Thy Shadows

As I release layers of my ego, I allow myself to be

weak and to crumble.

It's okay to not be okay.

It's okay to allow yourself to fall apart.

It's okay to be vulnerable.

It's okay to feel sad, angry, frustrated.

We feel it to heal it.

It's all part of us learning to let go.

The path of surrender and non-resistance is the path

that leads to liberation.

Each layer we shed and release, we move away

from ego and closer to Source.

Our true nature and essence is LOVE. There is nothing else.

We shed over and over again until there is nothing

left but pure love and light.

Listening to your body is a form of self-love.

Love Thy Shadows

Spirit only speaks through the lens of unconditional
love, forgiveness, acceptance, joy, and gratitude.
If your thoughts stem from any other emotion than
these, it is your ego speaking to you.

Love Thy Shadows

Loving yourself unconditionally is the greatest way
to show gratitude to the Universe.
When you remember and honor your divinity, you
tap into pure Source energy.
You are beautifully and wonderfully made in the image of
God/The Universe/The Creator/The Source.

Love Thy Shadows

Everything we experience and how we perceive that experience is a
direct reflection of our internal state of being in that moment.
If we truly love ourselves, we love everything and everyone.
If we are judging others, it is because we judge ourselves.
Whatever stirs you up is strong in you too.
Our reactions to others are a mirror into our own soul.

Love Thy Shadows

ou must first become **nothing**
Before remembering you are **everything.**

Love Thy Shadows

Life is an internship.

With each struggle or hurdle in life, we gain

new knowledge and understanding.

Without the hard times, there would be no growth.

We don't grow nearly as much when we are on mountaintops as we

do when we are at rock bottom and the only way to go is up.

Life on Earth is a giant internship where every moment and every

experience is an opportunity to learn and grow.

Love Thy Shadows

The healing journey is not all love and light all of the time.

No part of the Earth is light all of the time.

One side is shining while the other side sleeps in darkness.

Everything is cyclical, Simultaneous opposites,

A dichotomy, A balance of opposing forces,

An unsolvable riddle.

Love Thy Shadows

Some days it's hard to be human.

Some days it's hard to fake it 'til you make it.

Some days it's hard to exist at all.

Even the sensation of opening your

eyes can be painful and overstimulating.

Some days you wake up and you cannot wait to go back to sleep

again so you don't have to feel catatonic and useless.

These are the days where simply being alive is heroic work.

Love Thy Shadows

Remember that light does not exist without darkness.
We go into the caves and darkness of the deepest recesses of our
soul, and we bring in the light so we can see the truth.
Our shadows want to be brought to the light to be loved,
acknowledged, accepted, and forgiven.
Our shadows are there to teach us deeper layers and
truths about unconditional self-love.

Love Thy Shadows

We go bravely into the deep layers of our

darkness, of our shadows, of the ether.

We head into the black abyss of the unknown void.

We remember that everything grows in darkness.

The darkness is where we plant ourselves.

It's where we surrender our resistance.

It's where we crack ourselves open so that love and light can enter.

Those deep parts of ourselves that we don't want anyone to see,

Those parts want to be acknowledged and honored.

Those parts need love too.

We continue to shed and purify ourselves until there

is nothing left but pure love and light.

Pure Source Energy.

Love Thy Shadows

Your deepest, darkest shadow is the catalyst for the most profound growth.

The heart seeks to forgive the turmoil the mind has created.

Love Thy Shadows

Do not believe the thoughts about yourself when your ego is running
wild and your mind is in a tornado of memories of
past mistakes and past hurt.
Remember that you can see clearly to the
truth when the water is calm.
You can't see to the bottom of a river or stream when there are too
many waves clouding your vision.
Self-love is always the solution, especially when you are
riding the stormy seas of the mind.

Love Thy Shadows

Our shadows do not get enough credit for bravely standing strong
and steady in the hidden and repressed parts of our being.
Our shadows deserve the utmost gratitude for holding space for the
darkness we are not ready to face.
Our shadows courageously hang on until we are ready to
bring them love and light.
They have spent a lifetime being shunned by us,
But they continue to show up and hold space anyway.

Love Thy Shadows

Your shadows and darkness are the motor that drives you back to your light.

Love Thy Shadows

You're not always going to wake up feeling like the best version of
yourself.
But whatever version you are still deserves unconditional love and
acceptance.

Love Thy Shadows

The darkness inside of you may not even be yours in the first place.
Darkness, demons, and pain are passed down the family line until a
soul awakens and is brave enough to bring in love,
light, and forgiveness.
Facing the darkness head-on is an act of courage and bravery.
It is stepping into the unknown, the infinite ether void.
Even during your darkest times, you can still access the light of
love, acceptance, and forgiveness.
The darkness will continually remind you to tap into your light.

Love Thy Shadows

It's okay to fall apart over and over again.

It's okay for your heart to crack open.

It's okay to feel weak and vulnerable.

It's okay to not be okay.

Life will not always be easy.

Life will not always be rainbows and butterflies.

We are here on borrowed time in Earth school.

The struggles are here to help us learn and grow.

The valleys are where we tap into our strength.

We cannot fully understand pure bliss and joy without

understanding our own personal hell.

Love Thy Shadows

Shadow work is the deepest form of unconditional self-love and forgiveness.

Love Thy Shadows

Thank you to my shadows for holding the space
I was not ready to face.
Thank you to my shadows for sticking around until I was ready to
hear the cry of your repression.
Thank you to my shadows who bravely remained locked in the
darkness until I was ready to bring in the candle of love and light.
Thank you to my shadows for teaching me that acceptance and
forgiveness is always possible, no matter how dark it is inside.
Thank you to my shadows for teaching me time and time again to
remember my light.

Love Thy Shadows

Our shadows teach us that we can always open our hearts more.

We can always love more.

Our shadows teach us time and time again that unconditional self-love is always the answer.

Love Thy Shadows

The darkness is a blank canvas,

A void that gives you all the space in the world

To radically love and accept every part of yourself.

Self-love is our own personal superpower, and it's how we heal every molecule and particle of our multidimensional being.

The doorway to liberation is through the parts of yourself that you avoid.

On the other side of the storm lies clarity and understanding.

Love Thy Shadows

Be patient as you work through each layer of your multidimensional being.

There are many layers of the onion:

- The physical layer
- The emotional layer
- The mental layer
- The spiritual layer
- The subconscious layer

Each will present different wounds and challenges in order to help you grow and evolve.

Liberating yourself is a daily and lifelong process.

It takes consistent work and effort.

It takes bravery and courage.

It's painful and exhausting.

But each time you work through a layer,

You liberate your soul a little more.

Little by little, you shed and transmute,

Releasing what is no longer serving you.

Each time you release, you get closer to your true nature of pure unconditional Source love.

Love Thy Shadows

Underneath the tornado of turmoil is the remembrance of your
divinity.

No matter the storm you are navigating, you must remember that
you are pure Source love at your core.

When you tap into that truth, you are reminded that you are
unshakeable.

The storms are there to bring to the surface the parts of us that need healing.

Love Thy Shadows

The ego is not a bad thing or something to be hated.

The ego is a mirror into the parts of us that want to be loved, heard, acknowledged, and accepted.

The ego brings to the surface the parts of ourselves that need to be felt and liberated.

Our ego is a compilation of all the memories, emotions, and aspects of ourselves that we try to bury and repress.

The path to liberation is through allowing ourselves to acknowledge our shadow aspects in their entirety.

We say thank you for teaching us.

We allow you to be felt and healed with love and grace.

Love Thy Shadows

Our experience of life is a direct reflection of our internal state of being.

If our internal state is run by the unhealed parts of our ego, we will continually be presented with experiences and relationships that trigger our inner wounds.

If our internal state is run by love, gratitude, and abundance, we will be blessed with magic and abundance in our lives.

Whatever keeps coming up in 3D reality is a lesson we need to learn from.

We are constantly attracting experiences and interactions to help us grow and break cycles.

Love Thy Shadows

Each moment is an opportunity to learn something new.
Each moment is an opportunity to practice a
skill you need to improve.
Each moment is an opportunity to practice observation of the ego.
Each moment is an opportunity to surrender and accept whatever the
Universe has put in front of you.

Love Thy Shadows

Our energy is constantly changing.

We are energetically different literally every second of every day.

Nothing is permanent.

Everything is transient.

It can be easy to allow our emotions to take over, but we must remember that emotions are simply energy in motion.

Just like everything else in life, emotions are transient.

They are visitors passing through our vessel, through our home.

They stop by to say:

"Hello, I am here to be acknowledged and to show you where healing is still needed within. Will you honor my existence? I won't stay forever, as long as you don't repress me or attach to me. I will make my way through with love and grace if you allow me to. Really, it's not that hard if you step out of the way and surrender your resistance."

Just like clouds floating by in the sky or cars driving on a busy street, our thoughts and emotions make their way through our body and soul.

It is important to acknowledge and honor whatever is passing through your system, whether it be joy, sadness, anger, or resentment. All emotions have a story to tell, and they all deserve to be heard—even the painful ones.

The only true way they can pass through for good is if we lean in and allow ourselves to feel and honor them in their entirety.

Love Thy Shadows

Spirituality is being on fire.

Constantly burning away layers that are no longer serving you.

Releasing ties from past lives, parallel lives, ancestral ties that aren't

your cross to bear.

You chose to come back to heal and release all of these ties.

You chose to come back to be the cycle breaker.

You chose to come back and transmute your pain into wisdom.

You chose to come back to purify yourself.

You chose the more difficult path.

Nothing that's worth it is ever quick or easy.

You are in this for the long haul.

Love Thy Shadows

With each struggle or hurdle in life, we gain new knowledge and
understanding.
Without the hard times, there would be no growth.
We don't grow when we are on mountaintops.
We grow when we are buried at rock bottom, and the only way to go
is up.
Each time a new struggle arises, we can use the tools and knowledge
we gained from previous life lessons.
We have many tools in our toolbox to understand and transmute
these energies.
Life on Earth is a giant internship where every moment and every
experience is an opportunity to learn and grow.
We are constantly changing, shedding, and releasing old versions of
ourselves, making way for new growth and new blooms of our
beautiful soul.
Just like the trees, we go through many cycles of death and rebirth,
forever changed each time.

Love Thy Shadows

The fact of the matter is, we never know exactly when our shadow
work, samskaras, and ancestral trauma are going to surface.
Of course, we would love for it to happen when we are in a safe
space at home or during yoga and meditation, but that is not always
the case.
The scars and pain come up when they are ready to be released.
That's why they are surfacing.
They are coming up from a deep, dark place in our subconscious
where we buried them for a later day.
The natural state of energy is to rise up from our root to our crown.
So often, we make things harder on ourselves.
So often, we are the ones standing in our own way.
Our only task is to simply get out of the way so that the energy can
come up and move through us.
As it passes through, we allow ourselves to feel the pain and the
emotions that are tied to it.
We feel it to heal it.

Love Thy Shadows

We are multidimensional beings of cosmic light energy traveling in
a human vehicle in the classroom of life.

We are the star of our own movie.

Each day, we are thrown different plot twists to see how we will
respond.

Some days are smooth sailing, and others feel like a hurricane.

We learn to honor the turmoil just like we honor the peace.

Relax, kid, this is all just a play.

Love Thy Shadows

Healing happens little by little, layer by layer.

If it happened all at once, it would be like an avalanche destroying

everything in its path.

Instead, it happens organically, like leaves falling off the trees in

autumn.

Love Thy Shadows

We shed and release to the point that we are raw and naked.
We release layers of self/ego so that we become closer to our true
essence.
The more we shed and release, the more we remember that we are
nothing but pure love, light, and forgiveness.
We reach a point of such deep acceptance of all parts of our soul that
we welcome our shadows to the forefront.
We love ourselves unconditionally and we bring light into our
darkness.
We thank the darkness because, through the darkness, we remember
our light.

Love Thy Shadows

In the end, there are only three things we need:

1. Unconditional love
2. Unconditional forgiveness
3. Unconditional acceptance

Unconditional means without conditions. It means love, no matter the past you have or the mistakes you have made.

It means forgiving and accepting all parts of your soul, even the parts that are hard to face.

Once we can do this for all parts of ourselves, we can do this for all beings and creatures in the universe.

When we see ourselves through the lens of unconditional love, we see all of life through unconditional love and acceptance.

We remember that we are all one.

We are energy masquerading as a human.

We are all individual expressions of the Universe.

Love Thy Shadows

Only in the depths of my self-hatred and self-criticism did I find true
unconditional self-love.
Only in the depths of my own personal hell did I find my heaven.
Only in my deepest, darkest nights of sadness and despair did I
remember the power of my light.
Thank you to the darkness for being the dichotomy and the contrast
needed for me to embody and activate my light.

Love Thy Shadows

Our shadows do not get enough credit for carrying the weight of our pain.

For years, maybe even decades, our darkness waits patiently until we are brave enough to bring in the candle of love and light.

Our shadows are a part of us. They are like beautiful flowers waiting to be brought into the light so we can truly see all of their colors and details.

Our shadows remind us of the dichotomy of all things in this life: the two sides of the coin.

Our shadows remind us of our light, and they give the space and contrast for our light to radiate within ourselves.

Without our darkness, we would not know our light.

Love Thy Shadows

The spiritual journey is a never-ending marathon.

It's running up to mountaintops and back down to the valleys.

It's surfing the peak of the wave, knowing that what goes up must come down, and we may get caught in the undertow.

It's knowing that new hurdles will constantly present themselves in order to teach us, make us think in different ways, and learn new skills to navigate the path.

Earth school is where souls come to heal and release; to purify and liberate themselves from the burdens they have carried for many lifetimes.

It's where we come to surrender and accept whatever comes on our path.

It's where we learn to look at every moment and interaction as an opportunity to learn and grow.

It's where we come to remember that our true essence is love and light, and we came to let go of the rest.

Love Thy Shadows

No one can walk your path for you.

It's your soul's path.

It's what you signed up for.

There's no way to bypass or speed through the difficult times.

The only way out is through.

The discomfort you feel is growing pains.

Lean in.

Feel it to heal it.

Let life soften you.

Let life teach you.

It's important to understand and honor the dichotomy of the elements.

EARTH

Can be rooting and grounding, or she can rumble and shake us off our feet.

AIR

Can be a soothing breeze, or it can be a chaotic tornado.

WATER

Can be cool and peaceful, or it can be a tumultuous hurricane.

FIRE

Can be gentle and warming, or it can be fierce and overpowering.

ETHER

Can be a calm, silent void, or it can be a whirlwind vortex.

Just like human beings, the elements have masculine and feminine characteristics depending on the situation. All things in life have a balance of opposing forces.

Love Thy Shadows

The darkness gives me infinite space to let all my colors shine.

Love Thy Shadows

There will come a point when you welcome your shadows to the forefront because you know they will teach you how to activate more of your light.

Love Thy Shadows

Storms don't last forever.

They last long enough to teach us what we need to

learn in order to evolve.

Don't forget that flowers require rain in order to grow.

Love Thy Shadows

Our shadows will always lead us down the path to our light.

Love Thy Shadows

Sin is an ignorance of the unconditional love that exists in every living thing.

Every living thing on this planet is its own unique expression of the Universe.

Love Thy Shadows

If you feel like you are stuck in the middle of a pile of shit, then you haven't learned what you need to learn yet.

Life will keep you exactly where you are until you learn the intended lesson needed for you to evolve.

Love Thy Shadows

I dance with my shadows.

I allow them to speak their truth.

I apologize for keeping them locked away in the jail cell of my soul.

I walk hand in hand with them into the light.

The light of love allows me to see my shadows in their entirety,

spending time acknowledging each beautiful and unique detail.

Our shadow aspects are part of our infinite being, and they deserve

the same amount of love as our light aspects.

Love Thy Shadows

The mountaintops,

The valleys,

The hurdles,

The stagnant times—

They are all perfectly part of the path, serving their own unique

purpose.

Do not rush through any moment, or you may miss the pearls of

knowledge it offers.

Love Thy Shadows

I allow all parts of my soul to speak their truth.

I pay full attention to every detail of the words spoken.

I hug and support my shadows as they allow their

vulnerability to show.

I repeat to them over and over again:

I'm sorry, I forgive you, I love you, I accept you.

Love Thy Shadows

Self-love and self-care mean more than Epsom salt baths, essential oils, and yoga.

Self-love and self-care also mean:

- Saying no
- Unplugging from social media
- Walking barefoot on the earth
- Hugging a tree
- Speaking to the birds and the plants
- Resting as much as you need to without guilt

But most of all, self-love and self-care mean radical acceptance and unconditional love of all parts of yourself.

Love Thy Shadows

We can rarely understand the true magic and timing of the
events in our lives.
Sometimes we forget that we are Source cosmic energy
masquerading as a human.
Life is happening, and we are here observing and experiencing it.
Every moment of every day that crosses through our energy
field is meant for us.
It simply cannot be any other way.

Love Thy Shadows

You are not necessarily going to enjoy every single

chapter in your book of life.

But no chapter can be skipped or bypassed.

Each page needs to be read.

Do not rush through the book, or you may miss what life

is trying to teach you.

Love Thy Shadows

The spiritual journey is a lifelong marathon.

Hurdle after hurdle,

Mountain top to valley,

Up, down, and all around—

It's overwhelming and scary and beautiful all at the same time.

Love Thy Shadows

Every shadow has a gift to share.

Every shadow has a truth to speak.

Love Thy Shadows

We come into this world with every single ingredient needed to make a masterpiece of our life.

Love Thy Shadows

The paradox of the shadow:

We hear the word "shadow" and think it means darkness.

When in reality, our shadows lead us to a deeper activation of our

light.

Love Thy Shadows

Our shadows lead us to our gifts.

Our shadows activate our power.

Our shadows call us back home to ourselves.

Love Thy Shadows

As humans, we spend our entire lives running from our triggers.
We avoid certain people, places, or things for fear that they may
bring something up inside of us that is painful.
From an objective standpoint, our triggers are a compass and a map
that points us to where we need to go inside.
Our triggers will lead us to exactly where we need to
go in order to heal.
Our triggers are simply the key to the unhealed parts of our being
that are waiting for us to bring them love.
Our triggers lead us down the path back home to ourselves.

How do you know when you've reached a state of true
surrender and trust?
When your entire life as you know it is falling apart right in front of
you, and all you feel is a sense of deep peace and knowing that it is
all happening FOR you.

Love Thy Shadows

The darkness is a magical place of its own.

In the darkness, our senses are heightened, allowing us to see, hear,

and feel things we may normally miss.

The darkness brings with it silence and stillness.

It is in the silence of the black void that our creative magic happens.

It is in the darkness that we activate our true colors.

It is in the darkness that we tap into our gifts.

It is in the darkness where we remember who we truly are.

Love Thy Shadows

In the stillness and silence of the darkness, we can hear
the whispers of our soul.
We can sense the gentle guidance from Source.
We can feel the calm and rooting vibrations from Mother Earth.
Stillness speaks.

Love Thy Shadows

You must fully embrace your shadows and your darkness if you want access to your infinite light.

Love Thy Shadows

The wisdom attained during a dark night of the soul is worth more
than its weight in gold.
The darkness will teach you everything you need to know about life
if you lean in and allow it to.

Love Thy Shadows

The caterpillar goes into a dark cocoon before emerging forever
changed as a beautiful, colorful butterfly.
Every single time you go into your cocoon of darkness, new colors
of your soul will emerge on the other side.
The dark times are what activate your colors.
The darkness is where you remember your power and light.
Every time you go into the depths of your darkness, you will come
out brighter and more colorful than you were before.

Love Thy Shadows

A$_2$ R$_2$

Accept

Allow

Release

Receive

Love Thy Shadows

You have to find liberation in your dark times in order

for them to pass.

You must fully lean in, accept, and allow the dark times to happen

without resistance.

Only then will you fully appreciate the light.

Love Thy Shadows

Cliff Notes Guide to Navigating a Dark Night of the Soul

- Spend time in nature every day
- Walk barefoot on the earth.
- Talk to the trees and the plants.
- Lay down outside on a blanket and connect to Earth's energy field.
- Allow emotions to come to the surface
- Feel it to heal it.
- Allow your shadows to be acknowledged.
- Allow them to speak their truth.
- Listen to your favorite song or music daily to bring you back into your body and promote dopamine release.
- Take a break and unplug from all social media, TV, and technology.
- Allow yourself to sleep and rest as much as you need without guilt or shame.
- Show yourself unconditional love, acceptance, forgiveness, and grace every single day.
- Let life soften you
- The hard times are there to break us down and break our hearts open. Let them.
- Each morning, find something simple to be grateful for and focus on it.
- Sit or lie down in nature in stillness and silence. Just breathe. Just be.

Love Thy Shadows

- Write letters to yourself full of love and encouragement. Remind yourself that you will always be there for yourself and that you will walk through the darkness together.
- Accept, Allow, Release, Receive
- Accept each moment as it comes.
- Allow life to teach you.
- Release egoic attachments.
- Receive the gifts and blessings from the universe.

Love Thy Shadows

Gifts from the darkness:

Slowing down

Stillness

Gentleness

Rest

Sitting with your emotions

Time and space to heal

Time and space for introspection

Unplugging from the 3D realm

Space to focus on the present moment

Time to just BE

"Just breathe, just BE. I'll take care of the rest."

—The Universe

Love Thy Shadows

Self-love is the answer.

Forgiveness is the answer.

Acceptance is the answer.

Trust is the answer.

Allowing is the answer.

Breathing is the answer.

Being is the answer.

You are the answer.

Love Thy Shadows

A dark night of the soul is the Universe's way of redirecting you to your purpose and destiny.

Love Thy Shadows

The Universe doesn't respond to what you are doing.

The Universe responds to who you are being.

The Universe responds to the frequency you are emitting.

It mirrors back to you the same vibration that you are putting out there.

If you are vibrating at the frequency of lack or not enough, you will experience this in every aspect of your 3D reality.

If you are vibrating at the frequency of abundance and more than enough, you will see blessings continue to manifest in your 3D reality.

Love Thy Shadows

Ego resents.

Spirit honors.

Ego judges.

Spirit observes.

Ego resists.

Spirit accepts.

Ego fights.

Spirit trusts.

Ego is limited.

Spirit is unlimited.

Ego divides.

Spirit unites.

Love Thy Shadows

The bumps in the road, the twists, and the turns are all invitations
from the Universe to practice who you say you are.
Every plot twist is an opportunity to practice acceptance.

Love Thy Shadows

The dark times force you to sit in stillness.

They force you to just breathe and just be.

What a beautiful gift. ☺

Love Thy Shadows

Dark nights break us down until nothing but gentle surrender remains.

Love Thy Shadows

In a world that places high importance on speed and productivity,
we can easily forget the power of slowing down.
We can forget that we are one with nature.
There is a beautiful magic in just BEING.
The trees and flowers teach us this every day.
They are never in a rush. They take their time growing.
They go with the flow of whatever life puts in front
of them that day.
They weather the storms and show up even more vibrant and
beautiful after the rain.

Love Thy Shadows

Dark nights of the soul are like a forced shutdown and reboot from
the Universe.

Dark nights are a time to stop and re-evaluate where you are going,
what's working, and what's not.

Dark nights force you to shed all the baggage that you don't need
going forward.

Dark nights are the closing of one chapter and the beginning of a
new life.

The darkness takes us back to the simplicity of just breathing and BEing.

Love Thy Shadows

Dark nights teach us the power of meeting each aspect of ourselves with gentle curiosity.

Love Thy Shadows

A dark night of the soul is the Universe's way of closing down one
path and redirecting us to where we need to go.
Sometimes it feels like a swift kick in the ass, but it's also a nice
reminder that we are not in control.

Love Thy Shadows

Dark nights are there to strip us of everything we don't need to take with us into our next chapter.

Love Thy Shadows

The storms bring out our true colors.

The storms bring out our light and vibrancy.

Without the rain, life would cease to exist.

Love Thy Shadows

Dark nights crack our hearts open until nothing but love, acceptance, and gratitude remain.

The darkness provides the contrast needed for us to appreciate all the simple things in life.

Love Thy Shadows

Dance through your darkness.

Cry through your darkness.

Kick and scream through your darkness.

Sing through your darkness.

Above all else, honor your darkness.

Let it soften you.

Let it teach you.

Surrender to it fully and allow life to shower

you with blessings.

Lean into the darkness; it will take you to a depth of self-love and acceptance that you've never known.

Love Thy Shadows

You know the shadow work is working when you can look in the mirror and genuinely love and adore every aspect of yourself staring back at you.

The secret to navigating the darkness is surrendering all of your resistance and allowing life to surprise you.

Don't be surprised if you feel ill and exhausted right before you are
about to level up.

When you are working through heavy layers of darkness and
repression, you will feel all of the emotions as they make their way
out of your system.

This is a necessary part of the healing process, and like many things
in life, you may feel worse before better.

Love Thy Shadows

Sometimes there are parts of us that need to die and fall away.

Most people know this as an ego death.

A gentler approach can be more beneficial, viewing our wounded

parts with curious observation and love.

Rather than coming at them with an intention to kill them, take it as

an opportunity to practice unconditional love.

Practice the art of gentleness.

Softness can bend and mold.

Hardness will break.

Love Thy Shadows

There will be days when the healing journey will feel easy and days
when it's hard to get out of bed and function as a human being.
No matter what type of day it is, the goal is to show up for yourself.
Become your own best friend, your own cheerleader.
The darkness can make you feel isolated and disconnected from
everyone and everything.
This is intentional. The Universe is teaching you to go within.
Everything starts from within.

The "devil" is anything that disconnects you from full trust and oneness with the Universe.

Love Thy Shadows

Be careful not to fall into the egoic trap of the spiritual journey:

Always pushing yourself to be a "better" version of you.

Ego will make you feel like you are not enough and have you

constantly striving to be better.

Spirit knows you are already whole.

It's okay to be on the self-improvement path while simultaneously

accepting yourself for who you are at each moment along the way.

Love Thy Shadows

During your lifetime on Earth, you will go through struggles and
trials in order to teach you and help you grow.
There's nothing wrong with looking at the bright side of a situation
and remaining optimistic, but don't do this so much that you ignore
and repress the true emotions you are feeling on the inside.
Emotions are a normal and healthy part of the human experience.
It is only when we repress, deny, or attach ourselves to our emotions
that problems may arise.
We don't have to become the emotion and let it overtake us, but we
do need to acknowledge and honor its existence.

What is healing? I can assure you that it is not all crystals, yoga, salt lamps, and essential oils, although these can be helpful adjuncts to the process. The healing journey is not glamorous, it is not pretty, it is not easy. It is the hardest thing a soul can choose to do—to heal from and break patterns of dysfunction that have been carried through many lifetimes.

Healing looks like many days and nights spent alone, crying for hours in your bed. Healing feels like being so exhausted that your body cannot tolerate being vertical without spinning out of control. Healing feels like you were punched so hard in the stomach that you cannot breathe. Healing feels like pain all over your body. Healing feels like your nervous system is on such overdrive that you can't tolerate the television being on or light coming in through your window, where every slight noise or vibration you feel is a shock to your entire nervous system. Healing is closing your eyes to rest and feeling like you're spinning.

I can assure you that healing and allowing these feelings and energies to pass through you will undoubtedly be the hardest thing that you ever choose to do. Is it all worth it? Absolutely! Warriors are not made from taking the easy path. Growth and evolution occur during the hard times—the difficult life lessons. This is where you get to see what you're really made of. Does it suck when you're in the middle of it, feeling like you want to die and give up? YES! But just hang on a little longer, and you will get to see your true warrior colors shine. You will see that all of your hard work will pay off in the end. You will see that if you allow these energies, feelings, and emotions to pass through you without judgment, they will indeed pass through. They may pass through like a kidney stone, but they will pass through.

You will see that we are all made of a constantly changing array of energy and molecules. Nothing is ever permanent. Everything is transient. So rather than resisting life lessons, resisting the hard path, resisting the healing that your soul so desperately wants and needs, allow life to flow through you. Allow these feelings and emotions to pass through you. I will tell you that it's not going to be easy, but do it anyway. Nothing great ever came from taking an easy path. I promise you that in the end, you will come out stronger, wiser, and more of a warrior than you ever thought you could be!

Love Thy Shadows

There is a common theme about polarities in the Universe.

Your calling is your greatest struggle.

If you struggle with self-hatred and self-loathing, you will learn to love yourself unconditionally and help others to do the same.

If you struggle with anxiety, you will learn how to ground and feel safe in your body and help others to do the same.

If you struggle with self-criticism, you will learn to accept yourself as you are and help others to do the same.

If you struggle with speaking your needs and your truth, you will learn to speak up for yourself and inspire others to do the same.

You will lean into both polarities to learn exactly what you need to before moving forward in life.

Love Thy Shadows

There will be moments in your life where you will feel like everything is falling apart in front of you and you cannot do anything to stop it.

This is intentional. It's the Universe's way of pushing you to surrender and let go.

It's a reminder that you are not in control.

All you can control is how you react and respond to what's put in front of you.

When everything falls apart, it's the Universe letting you know to make room because better things are on the way.

"I'll take care of the HOW, you just focus on BEING."

—The Universe

Love Thy Shadows

The main life lesson from any dark time is the art

of surrender and trust.

A magical thing happens when you truly attune your vibration to the

frequency of surrender and trust.

You finally let go to create the space needed for the Universe to fill

your energy field with all of the blessings that are meant for you.

Love Thy Shadows

The darkness.

The "not so glamorous" side of healing.

The part that is often left out in discussions of the healing journey.

When people hear the word healing, they may think of yoga,

meditation, reiki, crystals, salt baths, etc.

But for those who are truly deep on their spiritual healing journey,

they know the depths of darkness it takes to reach the glamorous

side of healing.

They know that they must face their demons and darkness head-on.

They must feel and honor every emotion that moves through their

system.

They must love and accept every aspect of their being.

They must forgive others, and more importantly, forgive themselves

for past mistakes.

They know there is no shortcut and no easy way out to bypass the

hard times.

They know they can't substitute their way out of self-love.

They know the greatest gift they can give to themselves is full

presence in every single second of their human experience.

They know the only true way out is through, and that they are the

greatest masterpiece they will ever work on.

They know they have to give their full attention and energy to the

"not so glamorous" side of healing if they want full access to the

glamorous side.

Love Thy Shadows

Don't get stuck in a cycle of always wanting to heal the
next part of yourself.
There is time and space needed for each aspect of yourself to heal
and integrate within your system.
Be sure to create space for recognition and celebration of how far
you've come and each hurdle you have made it through.
Healing happens little by little, layer by layer.
You deserve to celebrate every little layer along the way.

The "devil" is anything that disconnects you from full presence in the moment.

Love Thy Shadows

We are all here on our own hero's journey.
We are all here to go through trials and tribulations
in order to learn and grow.
We are all here to turn our wounds into wisdom.
We are all here to transmute our darkness into light.

Love Thy Shadows

The darkness will uncover for you the deepest truths needed to heal
yourself.
What is hidden in the shadows and the dark parts of your being is
what is driving your behaviors and decisions.
It is only when you can enter into your darkness with gentle
curiosity and acceptance that you can truly see what lies below the
surface.
You can begin to uncover the aspects of yourself that you have been
fearful of seeing.
The darkness will force you to face every subconscious fear that you
have within.
It will force you to surrender and accept all parts of yourself.
It is through surrendering that you become free.

Love Thy Shadows

If you can embrace your shadows, you can liberate your soul from a lifetime of running away from yourself.

Love Thy Shadows

The darkness will strip you of all the things you use to try and
control your life.
It will force you to look within and acknowledge the repressed parts
of your being.
It will initially make you feel powerless as you lose more and more
control.
But once you learn to let go, that's when you start to fly.

Love Thy Shadows

At first, the darkness will make you feel like you are losing all of
your strength and power.
But the more you go within and face your fears, the more power you
will gain.
Each time you face a part of your subconscious, it will be less scary
and repelling.
You will begin to feel and realize that the dark times are an
extremely powerful place.
The darkness gives you infinite opportunities to love yourself deeper
and activate more of your light.

Love Thy Shadows

The darkness is there to teach you the deepest truth possible about yourself.

Love Thy Shadows

The darkness will strip you of all egoic attachments so that your soul is the one running the show.

Love Thy Shadows

The dark times will continually force you to let go of anything that is preventing you from being your true authentic self.

Love Thy Shadows

Dark nights of the soul will bring to the surface anything and everything that is preventing you from being in pure flow state with the Universe.
The more you let go, the clearer your path becomes, and the easier it is to dance in flow with life.

The greatest contribution you can give to this planet is showing up as your authentic self.

The healing journey is a daily invitation to show yourself
unconditional love and acceptance.

Love Thy Shadows

Your shadows are the path to reclaiming your power.

Let your shadows guide you to exactly where you need to go to

liberate your soul.

Every moment in life where you feel like you are being challenged or pulled down can be used as an opportunity to step into your power.

Love Thy Shadows

If what you are doing in life doesn't make you feel alive, then it's
not what you are supposed to be doing.
If what you are doing is draining your energy, it
is not meant for you.
If what you are doing brings you passion and energy, then keep
going because it's your soul's way of telling you that you are on the
right path.

Love Thy Shadows

Anxiety is your soul telling you there are unhealed
wounds on the inside.
Depression is your soul telling you that it's tired of the egoic roles
you have been playing.
Grief is your heart wanting to crack open so that
more love can enter.
Anger is your inner child wanting to be acknowledged.
Your soul is constantly trying to communicate with you
through your emotions.
Emotions connect us to our spiritual self.
Learning to transmute your emotions is how you can heal
yourself from the inside out.

Love Thy Shadows

Even if you have been on your healing journey for years, it doesn't
mean that you will never get triggered.
The triggers are there to guide you to where
the inner work is still needed.
Be grateful for your triggers because they
point to where you are not free.
They give you an opportunity to practice who you say you are and to
utilize all of the healing tools you have acquired throughout your
journey.

Become aware of your wounds so you can transform them into an empowered part of yourself.

Love Thy Shadows

When something happens in your life and it hurts deeply
within your soul, follow the path of the pain.
The pain will show you where the work is.
When pain surfaces, it is asking for your attention.
It's asking if you can explore the deepest parts inside of yourself
with gentle curiosity.
It's asking for you to soften and allow self-love to heal all of the
wounds inside.
The pain you feel will always lead you down the path of
deeper self-love.

Love Thy Shadows

The healing journey truly never ends.

It is a lifelong practice.

Struggles and pain will continue to come and go.

There will be times when you can transcend your ego and times

when it will throw its hands up in resistance.

It's all a part of your soul having a human experience.

It's about riding the waves of life without becoming attached to your

emotions or the experience.

It's about sitting back in the seat of awareness and observing

whatever comes into your energy field, knowing that it's meant to

be there to teach you in some way.

Love Thy Shadows

No matter your gender, you have masculine and feminine energy
inside of you.

Everything in this Universe has a balance of opposing forces, and
humans are no different.

Illness and dis-ease arise when there is an imbalance in the energies
inside of you.

If the masculine is overpowering, you will be good at asserting your
power and getting things done but may struggle with gentleness and
rest.

If the feminine is overpowering, you will be good at loving yourself
and self-care but may struggle with confidence and standing in your
power.

The goal is to reach a state of balance between the masculine and
feminine sides of yourself so that you can tap into the masculine
energy to accomplish your goals while simultaneously allowing
yourself rest periods so you don't burn out.

Secrets to navigating the spiritual journey:

- Sitting with whatever emotion comes up inside of you in any given circumstance
- Patience
- Gentleness
- Listening to your body
- Listening to your soul
- Boundaries with friends and family
- Saying no without guilt
- Spending time each day alone with yourself
- Rest and integration time
- Celebrating all of your progress along the way
- Surrender, accept, trust, and flow with life

Love Thy Shadows

It is completely normal and healthy to have boundaries with your
loved ones, including your earth family.
Family is important, but when it comes down to it, each of us is on
our own unique soul's journey with our own struggles
and hurdles to navigate.
We are raised in a society where we are told "family over
everything" and "blood over everything," but it's not uncommon for
our blood family to be one of the main sources of pain
and trauma in our lives.
You can do both.
You can love your family while still having energetic
boundaries to protect yourself.
It's not only acceptable; it's also necessary.

Love Thy Shadows

We have no control over when our triggers or wounds will surface.

We do have control over how we respond to what is surfacing.

We can choose to become engulfed and attached to the emotion that

is passing through, or we can sit back and observe the emotion as it

makes its way through our mind, body, and soul.

We can choose to play a part in our own suffering by playing the

victim and attaching ourselves to the anger and sadness, or we can

honor and feel each emotion and then truly let them go.

The choice is always ours.

Love Thy Shadows

There are polarities to every single aspect of yourself.

You can choose any aspect and see the light and shadow side of it.

For example, the aspect of perfectionism:

In its light aspect, perfectionism allows you to be attentive to detail
and create really beautiful things and experiences.

In its shadow aspect, perfectionism can be rigid and make you feel
like nothing is ever good enough.

Every aspect is a dichotomy; the two sides of the coin.

The goal is to love and accept both sides of yourself while also
finding the balance between the two.

Love Thy Shadows

Do not fear the storms that come into your life.

Rain is needed to bring balance to the atmosphere.

Crying is needed to bring balance to the emotional and

energetic body.

Water is needed by all living things in order to grow.

The storms are there to transmute and clear what is no longer needed

in your life.

The vibrancy of life after a rainstorm illustrates the magical healing

benefits of water.

You are not separate from nature; you are nature.

Storms will always come and go on this planet and in your life.

Each time a storm passes, you will come out of it clearer, more

colorful, and more balanced.

Love Thy Shadows

The heart is the center of our life force.

The body holds our truth.

The mind can be a powerful servant but a dangerous master.

Our hearts and bodies know the answer for us long

before the mind does.

In fact, the mind can actually come in and convolute an answer that

the body already knows to be true.

Listen to the loving guidance and truth from your heart.

Listen to the signs and signals from your body.

There's a reason we have a gut instinct.

Trust the vibrations you feel; energy doesn't lie.

Love Thy Shadows

Not every person you meet in life is going to be present in every
chapter of your book.

Some people are in the first few chapters and they disappear in the
middle of the book.

Some characters come and then go, and then come back again.

Some are there to teach us a very important lesson and then carry on
with their own path.

Every person that comes in and out of your book of life is there for a
purpose.

The goal is to honor and accept each chapter and lesson for
what it is.

Humans have a tendency to hold onto both good and bad
experiences and people through attachments.

As the wise Buddha once said, the root of all suffering is
attachment.

To be in true flow state with our book of life is to remain open to the
characters coming in and out of the chapters and being grateful for
what they teach us during their time in our story.

Love Thy Shadows

When things appear to be going wrong, it's an opportunity to look at
life through a different lens.
It's an opportunity to surrender control to the Universe and allow
divine order to unfold.
It's an opportunity to look within and see any conscious or
unconscious behavior that is holding you back.

Love Thy Shadows

There's a difference between resistance from the Universe and resistance you put on yourself.

The Universe will give you resistance to let you know that you should not be expending your energy on a certain task or relationship.

Your own internal resistance arises when you are trying to force yourself to remain on a certain path or relationship that is not meant for you.

Whatever is not flowing is being forced.

Pay attention to the path and relationships that are in flow state.

It's your soul letting you know that you are on the right path.

Love Thy Shadows

Where are you afraid to go within yourself?

What are you afraid of speaking?

What are you afraid of facing?

What makes your soul feel uncomfortable?

That's where the work is.

The discomfort leads you down the path of growth.

Lifting weights will initially break your muscles down and make you feel weak for a few days, but once your muscles have healed, it makes you stronger in the end.

The spiritual journey is no different.

The Universe will make you feel uncomfortable to push you toward growth.

The more you resist the growth, the more you will be met with resistance pushing right back at you.

Lean into the growing pains. Allow life to break you down and soften you. Release control and trust that it's all happening FOR you rather than TO you.

You will be amazed at what happens in your life when you let go and trust that it's all happening for your greatest and highest good.

Love Thy Shadows

Sometimes life will throw you such a curveball that your entire life as you know it is flipped upside down.

It is the most profound way that the Universe course-corrects your path to the highest possible timeline available to you.

I no longer fear my life dismantling before my very eyes.

I no longer worry when things don't work out the way I thought they would.

I no longer resist when life falls apart all around me.

I know and trust to the deepest level of my being that the Universe has a very important and precise plan for me that was written in the stars before I got here, and my only job is to surrender to my path and follow the signs put in front of me.

All of my greatest gifts came from moments of darkness.

It's not always clear right away, but hindsight is 20/20. There is always a hidden gift even in the darkest of times.

Our job is to find it. When you have reached a state of true gratitude for your dark times, the intended lesson has been learned. The darkness will no longer be a place you fear but a place you welcome with open arms because you know there is immense growth and power activated there.

Everything I learned about myself and about life has come from the darkness.

I am forever grateful to every moment of darkness that forced me to go within to love and heal every molecule of my multidimensional being.

Love Thy Shadows

The darkness is where I learned acceptance.

The darkness is where I learned forgiveness.

The darkness is where I learned to love myself unconditionally.

The darkness is where I finally knew on a soul level that I am

worthy of life and love to the deepest parts of my being.

The darkness will forever be my greatest gift of this human

experience.

Love Thy Shadows

We live in a mirror-verse.

Every person we interact with is a mirror into our own soul.

Sometimes we are meeting past or future versions of ourselves, and other times we are seeing our shadows through another person.

Anything we react to in others, the good or the bad, is a mirror into our own soul.

If we pay attention, what we see as strong in others is strong in ourselves too. This could be a shadow or it could be the light.

We are all one. There is something that gets activated in us through each interaction we have in the world.

Love Thy Shadows

No matter how difficult or painful it is, you must always speak your truth.

The repression of one's truth can lead to illness and dis-ease within the body.

This can manifest in a variety of ways depending on the truth you are repressing.

Repression of one's true self is the equivalent of betraying your own soul.

You came here to be your true authentic self.

You came here to speak your truth.

You came here to be unapologetically you.

If you are not honoring this truth, there is a high chance some form of illness will begin from the inside out to get your attention.

Our body is always communicating with us through pain, illness, or emotional dysregulation.

Listen to the messages you are receiving from your body and soul.

Let your spirit speak. Your higher self always holds your truth.

If you are not speaking your truth, you are dishonoring your highest self, and there is nothing worse than living an entire lifetime feeling repressed from your true purpose and potential just to appease those around you.

Ultimately, you came here to live your life for yourself, not for anyone else. This is not selfish; it is simply your truth.

You can still live a life of service to others, but you must honor yourself first.

Love Thy Shadows

Self-love is the path back home to yourself.

Self-love is the remedy for all of your dark times.

Self-love is what makes you shine from the inside out.

No matter the darkness you are navigating, self-love is always

the answer.

It is always the way, the truth, and the light.

Love Thy Shadows

You will always be rewarded by the Universe for
honoring your soul and speaking your truth.
Your soul came to Earth knowing the path you signed up for.
Your only job is to remember and honor this path and truth.

Made in the USA
Las Vegas, NV
04 March 2025

19041053R00089